THEORY TEST STUDY AND REVISION GUIDE

GRAHAM CHALMERS

THEORY TEST STUDY & REVISION GUIDE

Published by Outdoor Media Limited in association with Matador
Hollister Cottage, Coombe Lane,
Shere, Surrey, GU5 9TD,
United Kingdom

ISBN 978-1784621-391

British Library Cataloguing in Publication Data.
A catalogue record for this book is available from the British Library.

Typeset by Troubador Publishing Ltd

Contents

Introduction

Why a revision and study guide for the Theory Test? Well, because the other materials available to a candidate are not really fit for purpose when it comes to actually studying for the test itself. Sure enough, handbooks, websites and the Highway Code itself convey plenty of information – in fact a vast ocean of information – but they leave you completely on your own when it comes to organising this information into an effective summary you can study. Many candidates sink in this ocean of information, so we have constructed a life raft – this book.

In this book we use a study methodology that creates coherent summaries of the vast bulk of information relevant to the Theory Test. These summaries are in the form of 'study patterns' (also called 'mind maps', 'creative patterns' and 'nuclear notes'). There are usually two summaries per section and each summary contains topic sub-headings in individual boxes, each containing short sentences or words summarising the relevant facts. There are three big advantages to doing it like this. Firstly, the study patterns are very fast and easy to read and so can be read over and over again. Secondly, your understanding of a topic is enhanced by seeing all the sub-topics gathered together in a logical manner. The third and probably most important advantage is that the study pattern makes it easy to memorise the facts. A study pattern acts as a key to unlock all the information you have absorbed on a particular subject from various sources and it enables you to recall memorised information in an ordered and structured way. This saves an enormous amount of time and effort.

We are not suggesting that all other sources of information relevant to the Theory Test should be ignored. We recommend candidates read through the Highway Code at least once. We recommend candidates attempt as many of the questions in the Driving Standards Agency's practise question database as possible. Practise questions are freely available on the internet. But when it comes to revision for purposes of remembering the facts you need to know; when the test is tomorrow and you have left things a little late; when you are feeling uncertain or need to quickly verify a fact, then this book is a real lifesaver. If you tried to summarise the source material yourself it would take weeks, if not months, of effort. You save yourself all that effort by paying the small price of this book.

GRAHAM CHALMERS

How to Use this Book

There are 14 sections in this book, each one dealing with a specific topic. Each section is introduced by a short comment called 'The Essence'. This is intended to orientate you to the heart of the topic you are about to study. You read this first.

There then follows one or, usually, two 'Study Patterns'. These contain the summarised information relating to the specific topic. You read this information in a circular manner, proceeding from one box to the next in an orderly way. It does not matter which box you start with because all the information is of equal status and of equal connection to the central topic.

Just reading through the study patterns once will put most people in a position to correctly answer most of the questions asked in the Theory Test. Of course, the more you read through the study pattern, the more you will remember. If you are having trouble remembering facts from a study pattern, you might read through it armed with a highlighter. Highlight the key words and you will have a better chance of remembering them.

Each section ends with a short conclusion called 'Test Tips'. These highlight particular quirks relating to the type of question asked in relation to that particular topic.

Once you have been through this book, you should read through the entire Highway Code at least once. This is available online free of charge at www.gov.uk/highway-code. Then go through this book again until you know the material. Test yourself on a selection of practise questions available online free of charge at www.gov.uk/practise-your-driving-theory-test.

A Few Words on Multiple Choice Tests

In this type of test the candidate is faced with a number of alternative answers from which the correct answer(s) must be chosen. This is not as easy as it seems because often the incorrect alternatives are seemingly plausible answers and a thorough knowledge of the facts is required to enable you to select the correct answer. Also, your time is restricted and quick decisions are required. Keep the following points in mind when attempting the test:

Each question carries the same number of marks so therefore deserves to have an equal amount of time devoted to it. It is silly to waste time pondering the answer to a question you don't know and then run out of time to answer questions you do know. There are 50 questions and they must be answered in 57 minutes = 1.14 minutes or 1 minute 8 seconds per question. Work on 1 minute per question and if you don't know the answer within 1 minute, move on. You can return to the question later if there is time.

Read the instructions *carefully*. If you are asked to mark three correct answers you must mark all three to score a mark. Two out of three gets you nothing.

If you immediately recognise the correct answer(s) select them by touching the screen in the manner prescribed. Be sure, however, to carefully read the question and all the alternative answers to ensure you have not misread the question. The multiple choice format lends itself to trick questions.

Where you are not sure of the answer, it is helpful to work by a process of elimination. Discard alternatives that are obviously wrong, then those you think are probably wrong, thereby narrowing down the possible choice of correct answers.

If you have time at the end, go over your answers to ensure you have entered them correctly and to double check on doubtful ones. When in two minds about the correctness of an answer, it is usually advisable to stick to your first choice.

The Theory Test does not penalise wrong answers by awarding negative marks. If you don't know the answer and can't work it out, have a guess – you have nothing to lose.

Getting Your Driver's Licence

To get your driver's licence you have to go through the following process:

Step 1: Apply for a provisional licence.

Apply online at www.direct.gov.uk/apply-first-provisional-driving-licence.

Step 2: Apply for and take the Theory Test.

Do this at www.gov.uk/book-a-driving-theory-test, but only after you have studied the material in this book and have had some practical driving instruction, preferably from an approved driving instructor. The Theory Test takes place at your local Theory Test Centre and is divided into two parts:

The Multiple Choice Questions Section; and
The Hazard Perception (video) Section (known as the HP element).

At the Theory Test Centre you will sit at a computer terminal which has both the Multiple Choice Questions and the Hazard Perception videos loaded onto it.

In the Multiple Choice Questions Section you will be required to answer 50 questions in 57 minutes (i.e. just over 1 minute per question) and you must get 43 questions (86%) correct in order to pass. All the questions are multiple-choice i.e. several possible answers are listed after the question and you have to choose the answer(s) you think are correct. You do this by touching the computer screen where indicated. Apart from signing your name, you do not have to write anything down during this test.

After a short break of about 5 minutes, you will go on to do the Hazard Perception video Section (HP element) part of the test. This takes about 20 minutes. During this time you are shown video clips of various real life scenarios. Using the mouse control as instructed, you click the mouse when you see a hazard come up in the video clip. The sooner you notice the hazard and click the mouse the more marks you get. You cannot cheat the system by continually clicking the mouse – you get no marks if you do this.

This book is primarily aimed at getting you through the Multiple Choice Questions Section, but it will also help with the HP element. Generally though, real driving experience is necessary to properly prepare for the HP element.

Step 3: Apply for and take the Practical Test

A practical test can be booked online at www.gov.uk/book-practical-driving-test on any day between 6am and 11.40pm. It goes without saying you must be fully prepared after taking appropriate tuition, preferably from an approved instructor. The contents of this book are not irrelevant to the practical test. Who knows what situation might arise during the reality of the practical test and the more theory you know, the more likely you will react correctly.

Step 4: Apply for your full driver's licence

Send your Pass Certificate and your provisional licence to the DVLA in Swansea within 2 years of passing the test. They will issue a full licence to you.

Section One

ALERTNESS

The Essence:

1. WAKE UP!!! – This is not a joke.

2. An ordinary car is as dangerous as a machinegun. Used carelessly, it can be a multiple killer and countless thousands have been maimed by cars.

3. So, it is reasonable that the law insists you pay very careful attention when driving and avoid drinking, taking drugs, driving while tired or medicated or doing things that might be a distraction. They are deadly serious about this and if you kill or injure someone through failing to be alert they may well put you in prison for a very long time.

4. Alertness means being wide awake, concentrating on driving properly, seeing the hazards, observing the road signs and markings and obeying them.

5. Keep your wits about you and use your common sense.

Unwell/Groggy/Strong Medication:
Reactions slower
Unable to judge distance
Uncoordinated
Read medicine label/ consult doctor
NO driving!

Alcohol & Drugs
Drinking or drugging =
NO driving!

Too Tired:
= fall asleep at wheel = serious crash.
Open window for air
Take breaks – every 2 hours
No long stretches on motorway at
night (if tired, leave at next exit then
stop to rest)

Effects of Alcohol & Drugs:
(1) Reduced co-
    ordination.
(2) False confidence.
(3) Poor judgement.
(4) Reduced concentration
(5) Slower reaction.

ALERTNESS

Mirrors:
Alert driver uses all mirrors
regularly = observe
surroundings back & front
"Blind spot" = area not covered
by your mirrors.
Objects hanging from mirror =
distraction + restriction of view

Avoid Distraction:
No phones (includes hands free)
No loud music
No fighting kids
Don't look at accidents
**When in doubt – STOP
WHERE SAFE TO DO SO
and deal with the distraction**

Means:
Wide Awake
Concentration
See hazards
See road signs
See road markings

Alertness Questions:
Observation
Anticipation
Signalling
Reversing
Mirrors
Concentration
Distraction
Feeling sleepy
Mobile phones

TEST TIPS:

1. Its all common sense and you hopefully have some. Just think; "What would a careful and very wide-awake old granny do?" and that will get you the right answer.

2. Always take the conservative, cautious option. The adventurous, cheeky option is always wrong.

3. Some of the questions on this section are very long with as many as six answers to choose from. Often three or four correct answers must be selected. Read the question and answers slowly and carefully to make sure you understand them. Don't worry; one minute is longer than you think.

Section Two

ATTITUDE

The Essence:

1. Attitude is about your frame of mind when you drive, how you react to events and hazards, your ability to control your temper and your behaviour towards other road users.

2. In driving, as in life, it is your attitude that determines quality. A good driver always has a good attitude.

3. A BAD ATTITUDE CAN KILL!!!– The victim's life is ruined, your life is ruined - it is not cool to be in prison.

4. Just remember; you do not own the road; all other users have just as much right to be there as you do. Who are you to get into a "rage"?

5. You may think you are cool driving like a crazy person, showing off and terrorising the old folks. Everyone else just thinks you're an idiot.

6. Most young people would dearly love to be fast, skilful drivers. However attractive it sounds, this is a bad attitude. Aim to be a careful, safe driver instead.

7. Drivers with bad attitude do stupid, dangerous things and can hurt innocent people through their immaturity. Driving is for adults, not spoilt children.

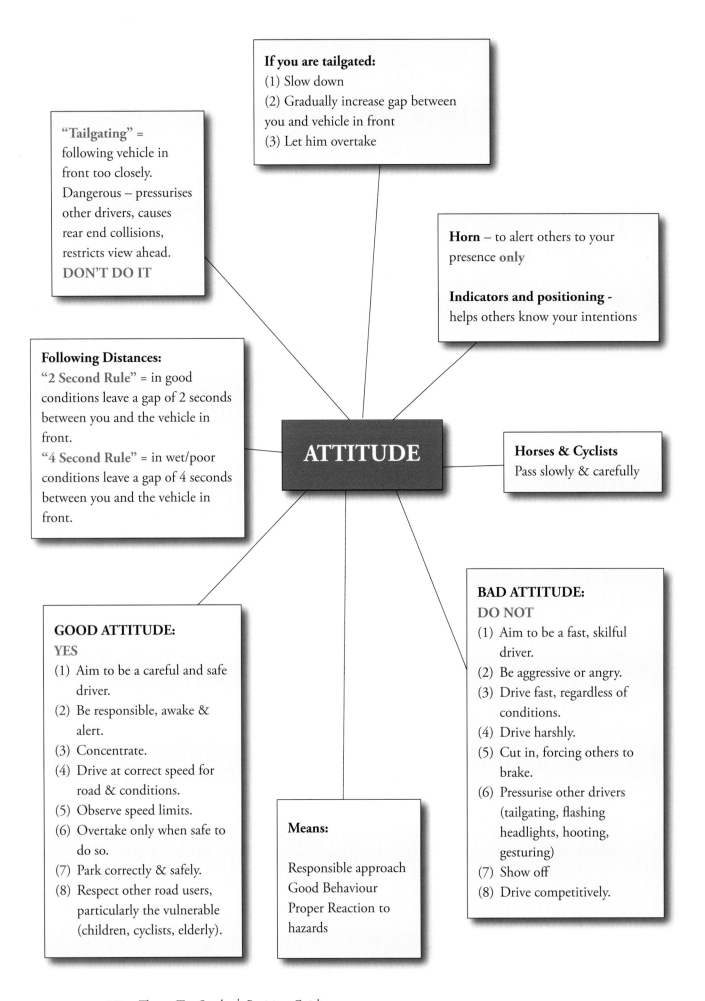

If you are tailgated:
(1) Slow down
(2) Gradually increase gap between you and vehicle in front
(3) Let him overtake

"Tailgating" = following vehicle in front too closely. Dangerous – pressurises other drivers, causes rear end collisions, restricts view ahead. **DON'T DO IT**

Horn – to alert others to your presence **only**

Indicators and positioning - helps others know your intentions

Following Distances:
"2 Second Rule" = in good conditions leave a gap of 2 seconds between you and the vehicle in front.
"4 Second Rule" = in wet/poor conditions leave a gap of 4 seconds between you and the vehicle in front.

ATTITUDE

Horses & Cyclists
Pass slowly & carefully

GOOD ATTITUDE:
YES
(1) Aim to be a careful and safe driver.
(2) Be responsible, awake & alert.
(3) Concentrate.
(4) Drive at correct speed for road & conditions.
(5) Observe speed limits.
(6) Overtake only when safe to do so.
(7) Park correctly & safely.
(8) Respect other road users, particularly the vulnerable (children, cyclists, elderly).

Means:

Responsible approach
Good Behaviour
Proper Reaction to hazards

BAD ATTITUDE:
DO NOT
(1) Aim to be a fast, skilful driver.
(2) Be aggressive or angry.
(3) Drive fast, regardless of conditions.
(4) Drive harshly.
(5) Cut in, forcing others to brake.
(6) Pressurise other drivers (tailgating, flashing headlights, hooting, gesturing)
(7) Show off
(8) Drive competitively.

TEST TIPS:

1. The correct answers are all about common sense and cautious, defensive driving.

2. Any answer where the driver takes no risks, is polite to others or anticipates some hazard is the correct answer.

3. If your parents would approve, it's the right answer. If your mates would think its cool, it's the wrong answer.

Section Three

SAFETY AND YOUR VEHICLE

The Essence:

1. In order to operate a vehicle safely, the driver has to know how the vehicle works. You must know the mechanical and operational basics regarding interior controls, steering, brakes, tyres, suspension, battery, catalytic converters, fuel and oil consumption etc. etc. If you are not a "petrol head" this can seem daunting and technically confusing. Do not worry. All the facts you need on these aspects are set out in "Safety and Your Vehicle (1) The Vehicle ". You will see the technical knowledge required is very simple and easily remembered.

2. The driver is also "Captain of the Ship" and is responsible for most elements of the safety of passengers. This is particularly important in relation to children. Take the topic of seat belts and child restraints seriously – it is awful being responsible for the death or injury of a child and the law will also take a dim view of you. Seat belts and child restraints are fully dealt with in "Safety and Your Vehicle (2) Driver Behaviour and Environment", which also covers topics relating to parking, route planning, vehicle security, crime prevention and environmental safety issues.

Tyres & Wheels:
Tyre pressure = check regularly when tyres cold
Under-inflated tyres = poor braking, poor (heavy) steering, increased fuel consumption.
Excessive/uneven tyre wear = caused by defective braking system, poor wheel alignment, defective suspension.
Minimum tread depth (cars & trailers) = 1.6 mm over ¾ of tread breadth.
Large, deep cut in side wall? = illegal, must replace tyre.
Unbalanced wheels = vibrating steering.

Fuel Consumption:
High fuel consumption caused by:
Harsh braking, accelerating, roof rack (wind resistance) carrying unnecessary weight, high speed driving (70 mph uses up to 30% more fuel than 50 mph).

Reduce fuel consumption by:
Proper servicing of vehicle, smooth driving (reduces fuel consumption by 15%), missing out some gears to reduce time spent accelerating (where conditions permit), reducing speed.

Steering:
Heavy? = under-inflated tyres.
Turning steering wheel when stationary = damage to steering & tyres

SAFETY & YOUR VEHICLE (1)

THE VEHICLE

Engine Oil:
Too much oil = oil leaks
Check oil before long trip.
Dispose of old oil at local authority site.

Head Restraint:
Properly adjusted prevents neck injury

Horn:
Do not sound in built–up area between 11.30 pm & 7.00 am

Suspension:
Press down on front wing – car keeps bouncing = worn shock absorbers

Brakes:
Break warning light stays on / Antilock break light stays on/ Pulling to one side? – consult garage for break check immediately.
If brake fluid level falls = possible accident.
"Brake fade" – caused by brakes overheating when overused going downhill – use engine to slow car.

Battery:
Most *modern batteries* are sealed *and need no maintenance. Old-style battery* – top up fluid with distilled water, to just above battery cell plates.
Used battery = toxic – dispose of at local authority site or take to garage.

Headlights, Windscreen & Seat Belts:
Must be maintained in good condition by law

Catalytic Converter:
Located on exhaust system. Reduces toxic exhaust gases

Plan Your Route:
(1) Allow plenty of time.
(2) Look at map or internet route planner.
(3) Contact motoring organisation if desired.
(4) Print out or write down route.
(5) Plan to avoid busy times for easier journey avoiding delays and helping reduce congestion.
(6) Plan an alternative route in case main route blocked.

Vehicle Security:
Reduce chances of break-in by removing valuables or locking them out of sight.
Reduce chances of radio theft by installing security coded radio.
Reduce chances of vehicle theft by:-
    (a) Parking in a well lit area or in a secure car park.
    (b) Installing an immobiliser.
    (c) Engaging steering lock when parked.
    (d) Etching car number on windows
    (e) Locking car and removing key when parked (even if absent for very short time).
    (f) Joining a car-watch scheme.
Never leave an unattended car with the engine running.
Don't leave vehicle documents in the vehicle.

Parking:
Don't park where cause obstruction eg. on brow of hill, near bus stop, where kerb lowered for wheelchairs. Parking lights must be used when parking on road where speed limit more than 30mph.

SAFETY & YOUR VEHICLE (2)

DRIVER BEHAVIOUR & ENVIRONMENT

Road humps, chicanes, other narrowing = traffic calming – reduce speed

Shoes:
Suitable shoes must be worn to maintain control of the pedals

Seat Belts & Child Restraints:
Driver must wear seatbelt if fitted – driver responsible.
Adult passengers aged 14 and over must wear a seatbelt if fitted (front & back seats) – passenger is responsible.
Child under three – correct child restraint must be used (front & back seats). Driver responsible. Only exception is taxi where no restraint available.
Child over 3 years but under 12 years and less than 1.35 m (4ft 5ins) tall – must use correct child restraint in front seat. Must use correct child restraint in back seat where seat belts fitted. If child restraint not available must use adult belt in taxi or private hire vehicle, or for reasons of unexpected necessity over short distances or if two occupied restraints prevent fitting of a third. Driver responsible
Child over 1.35 m (4ft 5ins) or 12 or 13 years – must wear a seatbelt if fitted (front & back seats). Driver responsible.

Environmental Questions:
Road transport = 20% of all emissions and causes air pollution, damage to buildings and consumption of natural resources.
"Environmentally Friendly" vehicle = reduces noise pollution, uses electricity, reduces town traffic (eg. Supertrams and LRTs).
Drivers help environment by:
Reducing speed, gentle acceleration, servicing vehicle properly, avoiding frequent short trips.
MOT exhaust emission test – to help protect environment.

TEST TIPS:

1. Many of the questions in this section have answers you either know or you don't know. For example, no amount of logic or common sense will tell you whether the legally required minimum depth of tread on a tyre is 1mm, 1.6mm, or 2.5mm (it is 1.6mm). These are things you just have to learn off by heart.

2. You might be asked about warning lights on the dashboard instrument panel. Make sure you know what they mean. For example, headlights on dipped and full beam, indicator is on, fault in breaking system, hazard lights are on etc. Actually get into a car and have a look at these lights. On most cars they light up initially when you turn on the ignition.

Section Four

SAFETY MARGINS

The Essence:

1. LEAVE MARGINS FOR ERROR!!! - In this context, a margin is a space within which you can compensate for an error before a collision occurs. The bigger the space, the more time you have to react to the problem.

2. In a collision, everybody is a loser. If you die in an accident that was not your fault, you are still dead. So, the margin a driver must provide must be enough to cater for other people's mistakes as well.

3. The main safety margin dealt with in this section is following distances (the space that should be left between your vehicle and the vehicle ahead so that you will not crash into it if it slows or stops suddenly). Closely related to this is the question of overall stopping distances (the distance within which you can bring your vehicle to a stop once you realise you have to – which consists of thinking [reaction] distance + braking distance). In turn, stopping distances are affected by the speed at which you are travelling and the weather conditions. Weather conditions also affect some other safety matters.

4. If you crash into the vehicle ahead, it is almost always your fault for not allowing a safe following distance.

General:
(1) When approaching a right hand bend – keep well left to improve view of road ahead.
(2) Most common cause of skidding is driver error.
(3) Coasting (travelling long distances in neutral) reduces driver control.
(4) Main benefit enjoyed by 4x4 vehicles is improved road holding.
(5) To control speed on a steep downhill – use engine as a brake by selecting a lower gear and use brakes carefully.
(6) Parking facing downhill – turn wheels towards the kerb and apply handbrake.

Safety margin = safe separation distance: The space you need to leave between your vehicle and another (usually in front) to avoid crashing into it if it stops or slows down or changes direction suddenly, **(about 2 seconds in normal conditions).**

Windy Weather:
(1) Side wind – most likely on an open road.
(2) Extra care passing pedal and motor cyclists – pass wide to allow extra room.

SAFETY MARGINS (1)

WEATHER & GENERAL

Hot Weather:
Road surface can become soft – affects tyre grip and braking.

Fog:
Use dipped headlights, allow more time for journey, slow down and increase gap between you and vehicle in front.

Icy Weather:
(1) Before starting journey clear ice/snow from windows, lights, mirrors & number plates.
(2) Trying to move off in snow? – use highest gear you can (prevents wheels spinning).
(3) Driving in falling snow? – brake gently & in plenty of time.
(4) **Note - braking distance on ice x10 normal.**
(5) On icy roads avoid wheel spin by driving slowly in highest gear possible.
(6) Approaching sharp bend? – slow down & avoid sudden steering movements.
(7) Steering suddenly feels light? – **Black ice!!** – ease off accelerator.

Wet Weather:
(1) **Note - braking distance in wet at least x2 normal (4 second rule).**
(2) Heavy rain – steering feels light? = aquaplaning – ease off accelerator.
(3) Gone through deep water (e.g. a ford)? – test brakes and dry them off by going slowly and gently applying the brakes.
(4) Motorway spray? – Use dipped headlights.

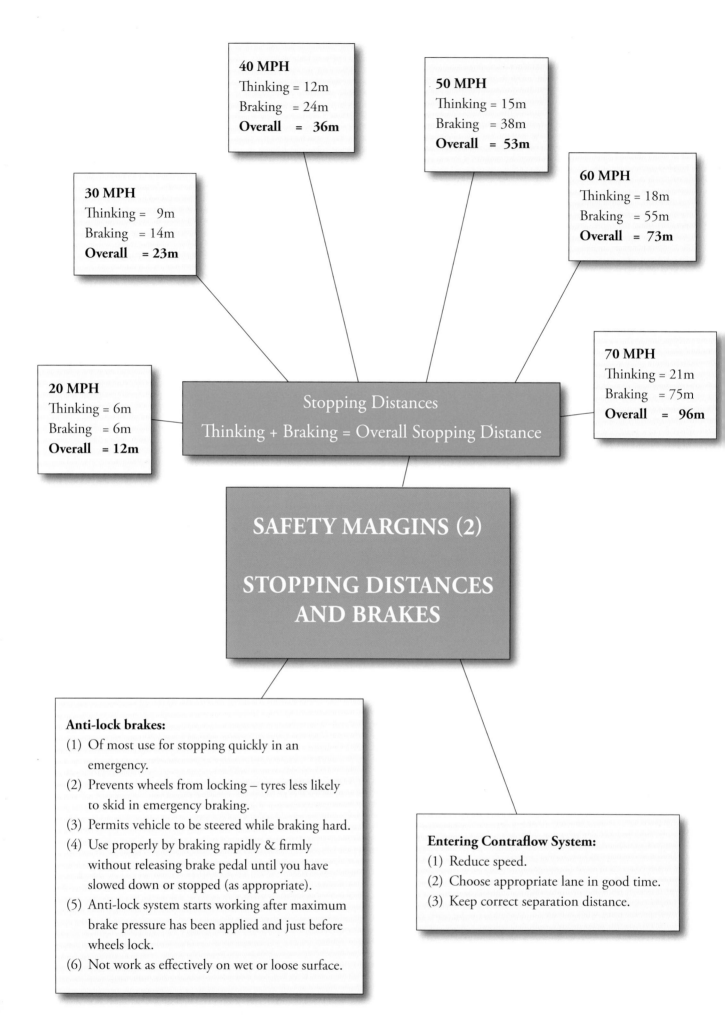

40 MPH
Thinking = 12m
Braking = 24m
Overall = 36m

50 MPH
Thinking = 15m
Braking = 38m
Overall = 53m

30 MPH
Thinking = 9m
Braking = 14m
Overall = 23m

60 MPH
Thinking = 18m
Braking = 55m
Overall = 73m

Stopping Distances
Thinking + Braking = Overall Stopping Distance

20 MPH
Thinking = 6m
Braking = 6m
Overall = 12m

70 MPH
Thinking = 21m
Braking = 75m
Overall = 96m

SAFETY MARGINS (2)

STOPPING DISTANCES AND BRAKES

Anti-lock brakes:
(1) Of most use for stopping quickly in an emergency.
(2) Prevents wheels from locking – tyres less likely to skid in emergency braking.
(3) Permits vehicle to be steered while braking hard.
(4) Use properly by braking rapidly & firmly without releasing brake pedal until you have slowed down or stopped (as appropriate).
(5) Anti-lock system starts working after maximum brake pressure has been applied and just before wheels lock.
(6) Not work as effectively on wet or loose surface.

Entering Contraflow System:
(1) Reduce speed.
(2) Choose appropriate lane in good time.
(3) Keep correct separation distance.

TEST TIPS:

1. You just have to learn the stopping distances off by heart. The principle is that the faster you go the further it takes you to stop and thus the greater the following distance you should allow.

2. Some people get confused by the difference between braking distance and overall stopping distance (overall stopping distance = thinking [reaction] distance + braking distance).

3. Questions are often asked about anti-locking brake systems ("ABS brakes"). These days they are fitted to just about every new car as a standard feature. The system operates when you slam on brakes and prevents the car from skidding on locked wheels (by alternately locking and unlocking the wheels). A car skidding on locked wheels cannot be steered and that is very dangerous.

Section Five

HAZARD AWARENESS

The Essence:

1. This is also about being awake and being aware of what is going on around you when you drive. The Hazard Awareness section expands the principles stated in the Alertness and Attitude sections by applying them to a range of hazardous and potentially hazardous situations. There is a great deal of overlap between these sections.

2. Drivers are forewarned of potentially hazardous situations by road signs, road markings and traffic lights. They are also forewarned by the behaviour of other vehicles. This allows drivers to anticipate hazardous situations in advance and take steps to avoid them or deal with them properly.

3. There is no difference between the expressions "Hazard Awareness" and "Hazard Perception" – they both mean exactly the same thing. However, "Hazard Perception" has become the name for the part of the test that uses video clips.

4. Real driving experience is the only way to properly prepare for the Hazard Perception video clip section of the test, but read this section before venturing out on the road so that you are properly oriented.

Other Cars & Drivers:

(1) Other driver makes mistake/ is reckless/leaves indicator on? – ignore it! Sound horn only to alert to your presence, not to show displeasure.

(2) Other driver annoys you? – ignore it, stay calm, take a break to calm down if needed.

(3) Involved in argument? – calm down before driving.

Cyclists:

(1) Cyclist turning left or right? – slow down & let him turn.

(2) Caution! Cyclists may swerve into road unexpectedly – give cyclists time and room.

Junctions:

(1) Reduce speed when approaching junctions.

(2) Blind Junctions/reduced visibility – take extra care, approach slowly, stop behind any line, then edge forward to see clearly.

(3) Keep junctions clear to allow other vehicles to enter or emerge.

(4) Don't overtake where there is a junction just ahead.

Buses:

(1) Stationary bus may suddenly move out into road.

(2) Passengers may unexpectedly cross road in front of stationary bus.

HAZARD AWARENESS (1)

Elderly Persons:

Driving ability affected by inability to react quickly.

Level Crossings:

(1) Stop before the barrier when red lights are flashing.

(2) The 1st warning of approaching train is a steady amber light.

Pedestrians:

When see pedestrians at crossing – slow down & get ready to stop.
Beware pedestrians stepping out from between parked cars.
Wait for pedestrians to cross before moving off.
Beware pedestrians walking towards you on blind bends.

Parked Cars:

Badly parked/parked in road = Hazard
Parked car doors can open suddenly.
Children can run out from between parked cars.
Cars may pull out suddenly.

Eyesight:
Must be able to read number plate in good daylight at 20 m. If not – wear glasses/contact lenses at all times when driving. Lose glasses? – No driving Tinted glasses? – Not at night. Ill health affecting eyesight? – Report to licensing authority.

Overtaking:
(1) Is a major cause of collisions
(2) **Do not if:** turning left soon/approaching junction/when view ahead obscured.
(3) 2way roads with 3 lanes dangerous – traffic in both directions uses middle lane for overtaking.
(4) Automatic gearbox – "kickdown" – moves transmission to lower gear for quick acceleration – helps in overtaking.

Other driver cutting-in?
Do Not –brake harshly/ sound horn/flash lights
Do – keep a safe distance.

Hazard Lights:
Only use when:
(1) Broken down and causing obstruction.
(2) Driving on motorway to warn traffic behind of hazard ahead

One Way Streets:
Start down one-way? – Continue on one-way
Do not – reverse out/ turn around in side road/ reverse into driveway.

HAZARD AWARENESS (2)

Drink/Drugs driving conviction?
= increased insurance premiums

Traffic Light Failure
– be prepared to stop for any traffic

Ill health affecting driving:
Report to licencing authority

Vehicle with amber flashing light?
= Disabled persons vehicle

Provisional Licence Holder:
Must not:
(1) Drive on your own
(2) Drive on motorway

Convex (curved) mirrors
= wider field of vision

Place names painted on road
= enable change lanes early

Lane closed on double carriageway
(1) Be wary of cutting-in
(2) Slow down & keep a safe separation distance

TEST TIPS:

1. Many of the questions on this section contain a photograph and you are then asked what you should do in the situation revealed by the photograph. This can be quite tricky because a photograph contains many details – so take your time, study the photograph thoroughly and consider all the answers carefully before making your decision.

2. Make sure you understand what you are being asked. For example, a question with a photograph might list two hazards and three non-hazards and ask you to select the two hazards as the correct answer. This is pretty straightforward. However, another question, using the same photograph, might list five hazards and ask you to select the two main hazards as the correct answer. The second question is much trickier to answer and there is the danger that if you do not notice the word "main" you might just tick the first two hazards you come across and move on to the next question.

Section Six

VULNERABLE ROAD USERS

The Essence:

1. A vulnerable road user is a user who is in greater danger than other users for some reason. All road users other than experienced, healthy, adult drivers (and passengers) in ordinary cars and heavy vehicles are considered vulnerable in some way. Vulnerable users therefore include; pedestrians, children, elderly folks, disabled people, motorcyclists, cyclists, horse riders, livestock, learner and newly qualified drivers.

2. What many of these vulnerable users have in common is that in a collision they are very close to the scene of the accident. Unlike the occupants of cars and trucks, they are unprotected by sophisticated bodywork incorporating crumple zones, safety cells, air bags etc. They are thus at much greater risk of injury or death.

3. Many vulnerable users also suffer some disadvantage that increases their risk of being involved in a collision.

4. Drivers must understand the different vulnerabilities of the various vulnerable users and compensate for these in order to keep these people safe.

Motorcyclists:

(1) Are small & hard to see, particularly at junctions. This is why they wear bright clothing and use dipped headlights in daylight.

(2) Turning right? – Check for motorcycles overtaking on your right.

(3) Slow traffic + changing lanes? – Check for motorcycles filtering through traffic.

(4) Unsure what motorcyclist ahead will do next? – stay well back.

(5) Windy day? Uneven road? – Motorcyclist may swerve – allow extra room when overtaking.

Cyclists:

(1) Also small & hard to see, particularly at junctions. Be extra cautious at junctions.

(2) Cyclist ahead is turning? – Give him plenty of room.

(3) Overtaking a cyclist? – give extra room when overtaking.

(4) Never overtake cyclist just before you turn left.

(5) Toucan crossing = light controlled crossing shared by cyclists & pedestrians who cross together on the same signal.

(6) Advance stop lines + marked area between stop lines at junction controlled by traffic lights – allow cyclists to position in front of other traffic.

Dazzled by lights?

– set mirror to anti-dazzle.

Turning right?

– Check for traffic overtaking on right.

VULNERABLE ROAD USERS (1)

Pedestrians:

(1) At night see pedestrian with reflective clothing + bright red light = organised walk.

(2) Turning left into side road at junction & pedestrians have started to cross side road? – give way to them.

(3) On country roads expect pedestrians on your side of the road.

(4) See pedestrians waiting to cross at crossing – prepare to slow down and stop.

(5) Amber light flashing at Pelican crossing? – give way to pedestrians.

(6) Stopped bus/ pavement blocked or closed? Watch out for pedestrians in the road.

Inexperienced Drivers:

(1) Just passed test? – To reduce risk of collision take further training.

(2) Be patient with inexperienced drivers & prepare for them to react more slowly and make mistakes.

Reversing

(1) Can't see? – get out & check

(2) Children are in special danger – watch out.

(3) Give way to pedestrians who wish to cross behind you.

Children:

(1) Ball bounces out from between parked cars? – slow down & prepare to stop.

(2) A school crossing patrol will stop you with a stop sign.

(3) Flashing amber light under a school warning sign? – reduce speed until clear of the area.

Horse Riders:

Horse riders in front?

(1) Slow down & be ready to stop.

(2) Pass slowly, giving plenty of room.

(3) If rider turning, stay well back.

Horse riders keep to the left, so at junctions expect riders to turn in any direction from the left hand lane.

VULNERABLE ROAD USERS (2)

Disabled & Elderly:

(1) Caution – their reactions may be slower.

(2) Be patient with disabled/elderly – allow them more time to cross even if traffic light changes.

(3) Flashing amber light on small powered vehicle = slow moving vehicle = disabled person.

(4) White stick = blind.

(5) Red band = deaf.

(6) Pedestrian with dog – dog wearing yellow/burgundy coat = deaf person.

(7) Wheelchair waiting to cross at zebra crossing – be prepared to stop.

Livestock:

Sheep on road? – allow plenty of room/ go slowly/be ready to stop.

TEST TIPS:

1. In any question regarding vulnerable users, the answer; "slow down and be prepared to stop" (or words to that effect) is always a correct answer.

2. Any answer that is correct for motorcyclists is usually also correct for cyclists and vice versa. They share the same vulnerabilities.

Section Seven

OTHER TYPES OF VEHICLE

The Essence:

1. This short section deals with some of the other types of vehicle you might meet apart from ordinary cars. All have some feature that either increases risk for themselves or for other road users. Drivers therefore need to know how to react to these vehicles and the special circumstances they create.

2. Many of the questions relate to long or large vehicles. These particularly increase risk to others because it is difficult to see past them and they behave in unusual ways when manoeuvring at turnings and intersections. They also create spray when travelling on the motorway in wet conditions.

3. Buses are long, large vehicles but additionally create hazard because they stop to let passengers on and off. Both the stopping and starting and the passengers (who turn into pedestrians once they get off the bus) require caution.

4. Other problems include vehicles that move very slowly, that cannot stop quickly or change direction or where the driver's field of vision is restricted.

5. Windy conditions make high-sided vehicles and motorcycles/cycles more vulnerable.

Long/Large Vehicle:

(1) Difficult to turn, particularly into narrow side roads - often signals left but moves out to the right OR signals right but moves out to the left before turning – stay well back/ be prepared to stop/do not overtake.

(2) When approaching from right, easily hides overtaking vehicles.

(3) More difficult to overtake because it takes longer to pass.

(4) Blocks view ahead if get too close behind - before overtaking it, keep well back to get best view of road ahead and only pass when it is clear.

(5) When keeping well back while waiting to pass, another car fills the gap – drop further back.

(6) Following in the wet & there is much spray making it difficult to see – drop back until can see better.

(7) Turns into road ahead and blocks both lanes – slow down and be prepared to wait.

Caravans:
When towing a caravan – safest to use extended-arm side mirrors.

Wheelchairs/Powered Mobility Scooters:
Driven by disabled/elderly people.
Upper speed limit (i.e. class 3 wheelchair/scooter) 8 mph.

OTHER TYPES OF VEHICLE

Trams:
be more careful because they cannot steer to avoid you

Windy Day:

(1) Vehicle least likely to be affected by crosswind = cars

(2) Overtaking high sided vehicle? – be wary of sudden gusts and allow extra room.

(3) Behind motorcyclist who is overtaking high sided vehicle? – keep well back.

(4) Overtaking cyclist/motor cyclist? – allow extra room.

Buses:

(1) Bus ahead pulls up at bus stop/is stationary at bus stop. You must:
   a. Watch carefully for pedestrians
   b. Be ready to give way.

(2) Bus is signalling to move off from bus stop? – allow it to pull away if it is safe to do so.

TEST TIPS:

1. In questions involving long/large vehicles slowing down, keeping well back, being prepared to wait/stop are always correct answers.

2. Sounding your horn, accelerating past, getting up close or passing on the left are always wrong answers.

3. When confronted by questions concerning a bus, assume that all passengers who have just got off are complete idiots who might dash into the road at any moment.

4. In questions about wind and high–sided vehicles or cycles/motorcycles, allowing extra room is always correct.

Section Eight

VEHICLE HANDLING

The Essence:

1. You have to know how to control your vehicle under the different circumstances you will encounter. Control is affected by things like the quality of the road surface (is it rough/smooth/wet?) by weather conditions (ice, snow, fog, heavy rain) and by the type of road you are on (narrow country road, urban one-way, humpback bridges, fords etc.).

2. Perfect driving conditions would be bright daylight on a wide, smooth, tarred road in flat country with no other traffic. Any other conditions require some adjustment to the way you use your vehicle. This includes not only technical matters like brake fade, wet brakes, engine braking etc., but also how you should behave in different driving conditions when overtaking, using headlights and in reactions to road signs.

3. "Coasting" is the dangerous practice of travelling downhill with your vehicle in neutral (or in a manual car, with the clutch pedal depressed). People do this believing it saves fuel. It is a dangerous thing to do. Vehicle design is based on the assumption that the vehicle will be stationary when in neutral, not travelling at high speed. The brake systems and power steering do not work well when the car is in neutral. The danger is obvious.

Rear Wheel skid?
Steer into it.
If braking and the vehicle is not fitted with ABS (anti lock braking system), release footbrake.

Steep Uphill:
Affects performance of car by slowing car down sooner & making engine work harder.

Single Track Road:
Vehicle coming towards you? – stop at stopping place and let it pass.

Rumble Devices:
To alert you to a hazard & encourage reduced speed.

VEHICLE HANDLING (1)

Overtaking:
(1) Overtaking on the left permitted:
a.   In one-way street.
b.   When vehicle in front signals to turn right.
c.   In slow moving traffic queues when traffic in right hand lane moving more slowly.
(2) Overtaking at night:
a.   Be careful because can see less.
b.   Beware bends in road ahead.
c.   Be sure not to dazzle others.

Coasting Downhill (travelling in neutral/ holding clutch pedal down): - is wrong because;
a.   vehicle goes faster
b.   less steering & braking control.
c.   No engine braking to assist.

Headlights:
(1) Well lit motorway at night? – always use headlights – only exception is when broken down on hard shoulder.
(2) Other vehicles just ahead? Headlights must be dipped
(3) Use dipped headlights during the day when visibility is reduced/poor.
(4) Dazzled by oncoming headlights? – slow down or stop.

Ford Hazard Sign:
4 things to note:
(1) Could be more difficult to cross in winter (ice etc.).
(2) Use low gear & drive slowly.
(3) Test brakes afterwards.
(4) There may be a depth gauge.

Using Engine to control speed:
To slow down using engine, change to lower gear. Use particularly down steep hills.

Snow:
(1) Do not drive unless essential.
(2) Chains are fitted to the wheels to prevent skidding in deep snow.

VEHICLE HANDLING (2)

Fog:
(1) Before setting out in fog, check lights are working and windows are clean.
(2) Leave plenty of time for journey.
(3) Reduce speed.
(4) In poor visibility (including light fog) use dipped headlights during the day.
(5) Fog lights (front & rear) may only be used if visibility drops below 100m (i.e. seriously reduced).
(6) Keep well back from vehicle in front – may stop suddenly.
(7) When fog clears switch off fog lights –fog lights are fitted to make vehicle visible in thick fog only & for no other purpose.
(8) Dangerous to leave rear fog lights on when not needed because;
a. brake lights less clear
b. following drivers can be dazzled.
(9) Parking on road in fog? – Leave sidelights on.

Stopping Distance:
Affected by:
(1) Speed.
(2) Condition of tyres.
(3) Weather (e.g. wet, ice etc.).

TEST TIPS:

1. Many of the questions on this section relate to the use of headlights and fog lights at night and in fog. Just remember that fog lights, both front and rear, are very bright and can dazzle other road users. Fog lights are only used in thick fog and must otherwise be turned off. Headlights on full beam are also very bright and are not used when there is traffic ahead because of the dazzle factor.

2. To make your vehicle visible to others in daylight conditions of poor/reduced visibility (short of thick fog), dipped headlights are sufficient.

3. Headlights must always be used at night, regardless of how bright the artificial lighting may be.

Section Nine

MOTORWAY RULES

The Essence:

1. Motorways are very dangerous places, so much so that learner drivers are not allowed to drive on a motorway.

2. One of the problems is speed. The general speed limit for most types of vehicle on a motorway is 70 mph and many motorists habitually go much faster. At speeds of 70 mph or more a collision is a very serious matter.

3. Another problem is congestion. In many areas of Britain the motorways struggle to cope with the volume of traffic, particularly at peak times. One of the consequences of this is that drivers feel frustrated on motorways, fail to maintain adequate following distances and race along far too close to one another. The result is multiple pile-ups, often with fatal consequences.

4. To deal with the special circumstances of this hazardous high speed world, special rules have developed to reduce the risks. Many motorways also have Active Traffic Management (ATM) systems. These involve overhead electric signs that communicate a variable speed limit and other information in an effort to reduce congestion and improve safety.

5. You should note that, except when crawling along because of congestion, one of the most dangerous things to do when driving is to stop on a motorway. There are special rules dealing with this.

Crawler Lane:
Found on steep gradients.

Prohibited Vehicles:
(1) Car/ motorcycle driven by learner (i.e. provisional licence holder).
(2) Farm tractors.
(3) Horse riders.
(4) Cyclists.

Emergency Refuge Area:
area on motorway for use in emergency or breakdown.

Hard Shoulder:
For stopping in emergencies only. Exception is in ATM area, when mandatory speed limit displayed above hard shoulder = hard shoulder can be used as running lane.

MOTORWAY RULES (1)

Joining the Motorway:
(1) Use slip road to build up to speed similar to traffic on motorway.
(2) Always give way to traffic on the motorway.
(3) Immediately after joining, keep in left hand lane.
(4) You in left-hand lane. Traffic joins from slip road ahead. You move to other lane.

Use of Lanes on Three Lane Motorways:
(1) Basic rule – keep to the left-hand lane unless overtaking. Left-hand lane can be used by anybody.
(2) Right-hand lane (i.e. lanes to the right) used for overtaking or turning right.
(3) Vehicle towing trailer not permitted in right hand lane unless there are lane closures.
(4) Overtaking on left only permitted if lane to the right has queue of traffic moving more slowly than you.
(5) Illuminated red cross displayed on sign above a lane – do not use that lane.
(6) Illuminated red cross displayed on sign above hard shoulder – hard shoulder for use in emergencies only.

Speed Limits:
(1) 70 mph in all lanes, unless otherwise signposted.
(2) Towing trailer? – limit 60 mph.
(3) Road works? = usually speed restrictions – obey limits.
(4) Active Traffic Management (ATM) = variable speed limits – purpose is to reduce congestion – advantage for speed to stay constant over a longer distance – reduces journey time.
(5) In ATM area, mandatory speed limit displayed above hard shoulder = hard shoulder can be used as running lane.

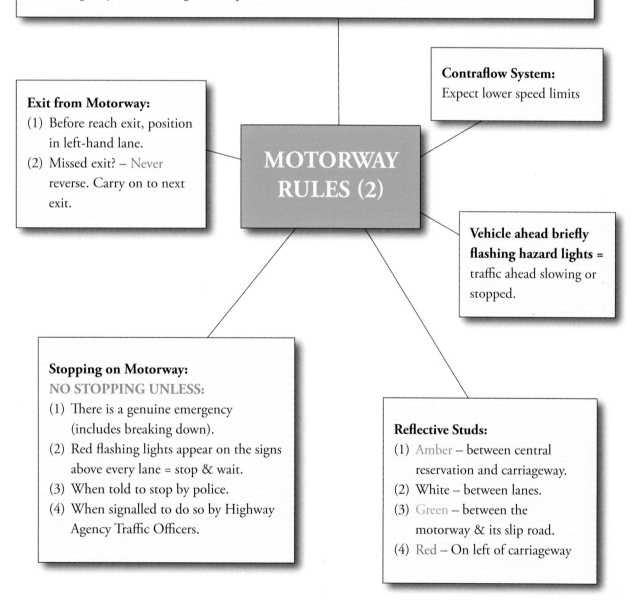

Breakdowns:

(1) More likely on motorway journey where continuous high speeds increase risk of breakdown.

(2) Pull off onto hard shoulder & use hazard lights.

(3) It is better to use emergency roadside phones than mobile – allows easy location by emergency services.

(4) If do use mobile – refer to marker posts to check position.

(5) To find nearest emergency phone always walk in the direction shown on the marker posts.

(6) When using emergency phone, stand facing the traffic.

(7) Emergency roadside phones usually linked to police. In some areas now also linked to Highway Agency Control Centre.

(8) Puncture? – do not fix yourself. Rather use emergency phone and call for assistance.

(9) After breakdown repaired, gain speed on the hard shoulder before moving out onto the carriageway (like entering from slip road).

Contraflow System:
Expect lower speed limits

MOTORWAY RULES (2)

Exit from Motorway:

(1) Before reach exit, position in left-hand lane.

(2) Missed exit? – Never reverse. Carry on to next exit.

Vehicle ahead briefly flashing hazard lights = traffic ahead slowing or stopped.

Stopping on Motorway:
NO STOPPING UNLESS:

(1) There is a genuine emergency (includes breaking down).

(2) Red flashing lights appear on the signs above every lane = stop & wait.

(3) When told to stop by police.

(4) When signalled to do so by Highway Agency Traffic Officers.

Reflective Studs:

(1) Amber – between central reservation and carriageway.

(2) White – between lanes.

(3) Green – between the motorway & its slip road.

(4) Red – On left of carriageway

TEST TIPS:

1. Although you are not allowed to drive on a motorway yourself, you should actually take a ride on a motorway with a qualified driver and look at the various signs, road markings and other specialised features referred to in this section. It will make more sense and be more memorable if you have seen it for real.

2. It would also help if you have done some driving on major roads or dual carriageways that, whilst not motorways, have many features in common. This will help with your grasp of rules relating to lane changing, overtaking and merging with other traffic at speed.

Section Ten

THE RULES OF THE ROAD

The Essence:

1. This section deals with the specific rules set out in the Highway Code relating to things like speed limits, parking, junctions, pedestrian crossings, level crossings and so on. There is plenty of overlap with other sections.

2. There is no big mystery here – you just have to learn the rules. You must read the Highway Code from beginning to end – but you revise from the study patterns that follow.

3. The rules of the road are all common sense measures to enhance the safety of all road users or are express conventions for the orderly management of traffic flows, without which there would be chaos. The primary rule of the road in the UK is that drivers drive on the left-hand side of the road.

Speed Limits (for cars/motorcycles):
(1) Double carriageway roads = 70mph
(2) Single carriageway roads = 60mph
(3) Towing caravan/trailer = 60mph
(4) Street Lighting? = 30mph
(5) Roadworks? = temporary speed limits – observe at all times.

Roundabouts:
(1) When going straight ahead, indicate left just after you pass the exit before the one you will take (i.e. before you leave the roundabout).
(2) Horse riders, long vehicles & cyclists may take unusual course at roundabout – beware!

Overtaking:
(1) Not sure it is safe? – do not overtake!
(2) On three lane dual carriageway – right hand lane is for overtaking & turning right.
(3) Can overtake on either left or right on one-way street.

Clearways =
no stopping at any time.
Urban Clearways =
no stopping during time of operation except to pick up or put down passengers.

RULES OF THE ROAD (1)

Cycle Lanes:-
(1) Solid white line = do not drive in that lane
(2) Broken white line = do not drive in lane or park in lane unless unavoidable.

Footpaths:
May drive over to get into property.

Parking:
(1) Do **not** park;
   a. near school entrance;
   b. at or near bus stop;
   c. within 10 m of a junction
   d. near brow of hill;
   e. on right hand side of road at night (except on one-way street).
   f. In disabled bays, unless you have a permit (blue badge).
(2) When parking at night on road with speed limit above 30 mph must switch on parking lights.
(3) Safest place to park is garage. Well lit area also good.

Unmarked Crossroads
No one has priority at an unmarked crossroads.

Junctions - approaching junction – realise too late you in wrong lane – continue in lane through junction

Yellow Box Junction:
May only enter when your exit road is clear. May wait in junction for oncoming traffic to pass before turning right.

Stopping:

Must stop when:

(1) Signalled to do so by police or traffic officer or school crossing patrol.

(2) At red traffic light.

(3) In accident where damage or injury is caused.

Turning Right:

(1) You are turning right & oncoming driver is turning right – normally safer to keep the other vehicle to your right and turn behind it (offside to offside).

(2) Dual carriageway with very narrow central reservation? – wait until road is clear in both directions before turning right.

Obstructions:

If obstruction is on your side of the road **you** give way to oncoming traffic

Turning Left:

When intending to turn left off main road into minor road keep *well to the left* on approach to the turning.

Headlights:

(1) Must use at night even in well lit areas so as to be more easily seen.

(2) When vehicle overtakes you, dip your headlights as soon as the vehicle has passed.

RULES OF THE ROAD (2)

Wrong direction?

Do not make "U" turns or reverse into busy main roads – turn around in side road.

Narrow Road?

Pull into passing place on left to let oncoming car pass.

Level Crossings:

(1) Train has passed but lights keep flashing? – You must continue waiting.

(2) Light s come on and bell rings while you are driving over crossing – keep going and clear the crossing.

Pedestrian Crossings:-

(1) *Zebra Crossing* – if pedestrian is standing on pavement waiting to cross, you should normally stop, wait patiently & let them cross (actual rule is that you only obliged to stop once pedestrian has moved onto the crossing).

(2) *Toucan Crossing* – shared by both cyclists and pedestrians who cross together – beware cyclists riding across.

(3) *Pelican Crossing* – Amber flashing light? – give way to pedestrians still on the crossing.

Reversing:

(1) May remove seatbelt.

(2) Do not reverse for longer than necessary.

(3) Not sure it is safe? – Get out and check.

(4) Never reverse from a side road into a main road.

(5) When reversing into a side road, greatest danger to other traffic is when front of vehicle swings out.

TEST TIPS:

1. Some of the stuff in this section you just have to learn off by heart. No amount of logic or understanding will help you work out what speed limits parliament has decided to set on various types of road. Speed limits are something you either know or you don't.

2. When learning something off by heart it often helps to try and reduce whatever you have to learn to the absolute minimum number of letters/figures that still allows you to remember the facts. Take for example speed limits. They are set out in Rules of the Road (1) above as follows:

Speed Limits (for cars/motorcycles)
(1) Double carriageway roads   =70mph
(2) Single carriageway roads   =60mph
(3) Towing caravan/trailer   =60mph
(4) Street lighting?   =30mph
(5) Road works? = temporary speed limits – observe at all times.

This is already fairly well compressed, but if you were having problems remembering the limits it could be further compressed into:

DC   = 70
SC   = 60
Tow   = 60
SL   = 30

Point (5) about road works is something you will remember without memorizing anything off by heart.

3. Mnemonics (devices to help memory) can also help, no matter how silly – for example the above might be more easily remembered by some as: diddly cat 7, silly cat 6, tow cat 6, silly lion 3. If you can remember this silly sentence, then you can work back to the speed limits very easily and hey, what do you know – you have remembered them!

4. Sometimes just the process of working out the mnemonic results in your remembering the facts.

Section Eleven

ROAD AND TRAFFIC SIGNS

The Essence:

1. You just have to know these, so it's more learning off by heart. Even the Highway Code does not contain all the road signs used in the United Kingdom, but all the ones you really need to know are set out here.

2. Note that in general, signs in circles give orders, signs in triangles give warnings and signs in rectangles give information.

3. Road markings painted onto the surface of the road serve the same purpose as road signs – to give orders, to warn you and to give information. These too must simply be learned off by heart.

4. The traffic and road signs illustrated in the following pages are reproduced from the Highway Code. The rules referred to in some of the annotations are the rules set out in the Highway Code. Read these rules.

(Illustrations contain public sector information licenced under the Open Government Licence v2.0.)

Traffic signs

Signs giving orders

Signs with red circles are mostly prohibitive.
Plates below signs qualify their message.

Entry to
20 mph zone

End of
20 mph zone

Maximum
speed

National speed
limit applies

School crossing
patrol

Stop and
give way

Give way to
traffic on
major road

Manually operated temporary
STOP and GO signs

No entry for
vehicular traffic

No vehicles
except bicycles
being pushed

No cycling

No motor
vehicles

No buses
(over 8
passenger
seats)

No
overtaking

No
towed
caravans

No vehicles
carrying
explosives

No vehicle or
combination of
vehicles over
length shown

No vehicles
over
height shown

No vehicles
over
width shown

Give priority to
vehicles from
opposite
direction

No right turn

No left turn

No
U-turns

No goods
vehicles
over maximum
gross weight
shown (in
tonnes)
except for
loading
and unloading

Note: Although The Highway Code shows many of the signs commonly in use, a comprehensive explanation of our signing system is given in the Department's booklet Know Your Traffic Signs, which is on sale at booksellers. The booklet also illustrates and explains the vast majority of signs the road user is likely to encounter. The signs illustrated in The Highway Code are not all drawn to the same scale. In Wales, bilingual versions of some signs are used including Welsh and English versions of place names. Some older designs of signs may still be seen on the roads.

WEAK BRIDGE

No vehicles over maximum gross weight shown (in tonnes)

Parking restricted to permit holders

No stopping during period indicated except for buses

No stopping during times shown except for as long as necessary to set down or pick up passengers

No waiting

No stopping (Clearway)

Signs with blue circles but no red border mostly give positive instruction.

Ahead only

Turn left ahead (right if symbol reversed)

Turn left (right if symbol reversed)

Keep left (right if symbol reversed)

Vehicles may pass either side to reach same destination

Mini-roundabout (roundabout circulation - give way to vehicles from the immediate right)

Route to be used by pedal cycles only

Segregated pedal cycle and pedestrian route

Minimum speed

End of minimum speed

Buses and cycles only

Trams only

Pedestrian crossing point over tramway

One-way traffic (note: compare circular 'Ahead only' sign)

With-flow bus and cycle lane

Contra-flow bus lane

With-flow pedal cycle lane

Warning signs

Mostly triangular

Distance to 'STOP' line ahead

Dual carriageway ends

Road narrows on right (left if symbol reversed)

Road narrows on both sides

Distance to 'Give Way' line ahead

Crossroads

Junction on bend ahead

T-junction with priority over vehicles from the right

Staggered junction

Traffic merging from left ahead

The priority through route is indicated by the broader line.

Double bend first to left (symbol may be reversed)

Bend to right (or left if symbol reversed)

Roundabout

Uneven road

Plate below some signs

Two-way traffic crosses one-way road

Two-way traffic straight ahead

Opening or swing bridge ahead

Low-flying aircraft or sudden aircraft noise

Falling or fallen rocks

Traffic signals not in use

Traffic signals

Slippery road

Steep hill downwards

Steep hill upwards

Gradients may be shown as a ratio i.e. 20% = 1:5

Tunnel ahead

Trams crossing ahead

Level crossing with barrier or gate ahead

Level crossing without barrier or gate ahead

Level crossing without barrier

School crossing
patrol ahead
(some signs
have amber
lights which flash
when crossings
are in use)

Frail (or blind or
disabled if shown)
pedestrians likely to
cross road ahead

Pedestrians
in road ahead

Zebra
crossing

Overhead electric
cable; plate
indicates
maximum height
of vehicles which
can pass safely

Available width of
headroom indicated

Sharp deviation of route
to left (or right if
chevrons reversed)

Light signals
ahead at level
crossing, airfield
or bridge

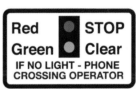

Miniature warning lights
at level crossings

Cattle

Wild animals

Wild horses
or ponies

Accompanied
horses or
ponies

Cycle route
ahead

Risk of ice

Traffic queues
likely ahead

Distance over
which road
humps extend

Other danger;
plate indicates
nature of
danger

Soft verges

Side winds

Hump bridge

Worded warning
sign

Quayside or
river bank

Risk of
grounding

Direction signs

Mostly rectangular

Signs on motorways - blue backgrounds

At a junction leading directly
into a motorway (junction
number may be shown
on a black background)

On approaches to
junctions (junction number
on black background)

Route confirmatory
sign after junction

Downward pointing arrows mean 'Get in lane'
The left-hand lane leads to a different destination from the other lanes.

The panel with the inclined arrow indicates the destinations which can be reached
by leaving the motorway at the next junction

Signs on primary routes - green backgrounds

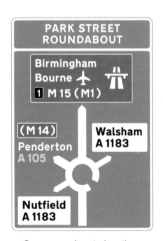

On approaches to junctions

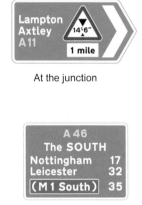

At the junction

Route confirmatory
sign after junction

On approaches
to junctions

On approach to a junction
in Wales (bilingual)

Blue panels indicate that the motorway starts at the junction ahead.
Motorways shown in brackets can also be reached along the route indicated.
White panels indicate local or non-primary routes leading from the junction ahead.
Brown panels show the route to tourist attractions.
The name of the junction may be shown at the top of the sign.
The aircraft symbol indicates the route to an airport.
A symbol may be included to warn of a hazard or restriction along that route.

Primary route forming
part of a ring road

Signs on non-primary and local routes - black borders

On approaches to junctions

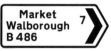

At the junction

Direction to toilets
with access for the
disabled

Green panels indicate that the primary route starts at the junction ahead.
Route numbers on a blue background show the direction to a motorway.
Route numbers on a green background show the direction to a primary route.

Other direction signs

Picnic site

Ancient monument in the care
of English Heritage

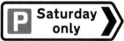

Direction to a car park

Tourist attraction

Direction to camping
and caravan site

Advisory route for lorries

Route for pedal
cycles forming part
of a network

Recommended route for
pedal cycles to place shown

Route for pedestrians

Symbols showing emergency diversion
route for motorway and other main road traffic

Diversion route

Information signs

All rectangular

Entrance to controlled parking zone

Entrance to congestion charging zone

End of controlled parking zone

Advance warning of restriction or prohibition ahead

Parking place for solo motorcycles

With-flow bus lane ahead which pedal cycles and taxis may also use

Lane designated for use by high occupancy vehicles (HOV) - see rule 142

Vehicles permitted to use an HOV lane ahead

End of motorway

Start of motorway and point from which motorway regulations apply

Appropriate traffic lanes at junction ahead

Traffic on the main carriageway coming from right has priority over joining traffic

Additional traffic joining from left ahead. Traffic on main carriageway has priority over joining traffic from right hand lane of slip road

Traffic in right hand lane of slip road joining the main carriageway has priority over left hand lane

'Countdown' markers at exit from motorway (each bar represents 100 yards to the exit). Green-backed markers may be used on primary routes and white-backed markers with black bars on other routes. At approaches to concealed level crossings white-backed markers with red bars may be used. Although these will be erected at equal distances the bars do not represent 100 yard intervals.

Motorway service area sign showing the operator's name

Traffic has priority over
oncoming vehicles

Hospital ahead with
Accident and
Emergency facilities

Tourist
information
point

No through road
for vehicles

Recommended route
for pedal cycles

Home Zone Entry

Area in which
cameras are
used to enforce
traffic regulations

Bus lane on road at
junction ahead

Road works signs

Road works

Loose
chippings

Temporary hazard
at road works

Temporary lane closure
(the number and position
of arrows and red bars
may be varied according
to lanes open and closed)

Slow-moving or
stationary works
vehicle blocking a
traffic lane. Pass in
the direction shown
by the arrow.

Mandatory
speed
limit ahead

Road works
1 mile ahead

End of road works and
any temporary restrictions
including speed limits

Signs used on the back of slow-moving or
stationary vehicles warning of a lane closed
ahead by a works vehicle. There are no
cones on the road.

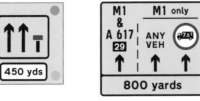

Lane restrictions at
road works ahead

One lane crossover
at contraflow
road works

Road markings

Across the carriageway

Stop line at signals or
police control

Stop line at 'Stop' sign

Stop line for pedestrians
at a level crossing

Give way to traffic on major road
(can also be used at
mini roundabouts)

Give way to traffic from the right
at a roundabout

Give way to traffic from the right
at a mini-roundabout

Along the carriageway

Edge line

Centre line
See Rule 127

Hazard
warning line
See Rule 127

Double white lines
See Rules 128 and 129

See Rule 130

Lane line See
Rule 131

Along the edge of the carriageway

Waiting restrictions

Waiting restrictions indicated by yellow lines apply to the carriageway, pavement and verge. You may stop to load or unload (unless there are also loading restrictions as described below) or while passengers board or alight. Double yellow lines mean no waiting at any time, unless there are signs that specifically indicate seasonal restrictions. The times at which the restrictions apply for other road markings are shown on nearby plates or on entry signs to controlled parking zones. If no days are shown on the signs, the restrictions are in force every day including Sundays and Bank Holidays. White bay markings and upright signs (see below) indicate where parking is allowed.

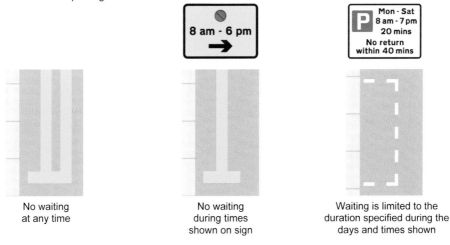

No waiting
at any time

No waiting
during times
shown on sign

Waiting is limited to the
duration specified during the
days and times shown

Red Route stopping controls

Red lines are used on some roads instead of yellow lines. In London the double and single red lines used on Red Routes indicate that stopping to park, load/unload or to board and alight from a vehicle (except for a licensed taxi or if you hold a Blue Badge) is prohibited. The red lines apply to the carriageway, pavement and verge. The times that the red line prohibitions apply are shown on nearby signs, but the double red line ALWAYS means no stopping at any time. On Red Routes you may stop to park, load/unload in specially marked boxes and adjacent signs specify the times and purposes and duration allowed. A box MARKED IN RED indicates that it may only be available for the purpose specified for part of the day (eg between busy peak periods). A box MARKED IN WHITE means that it is available throughout the day.

RED AND SINGLE YELLOW LINES CAN ONLY GIVE A GUIDE TO THE RESTRICTIONS AND CONTROLS IN FORCE AND SIGNS, NEARBY OR AT A ZONE ENTRY, MUST BE CONSULTED.

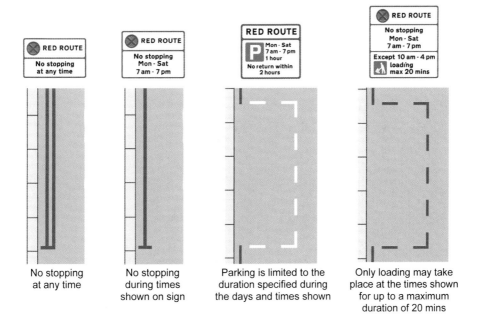

No stopping
at any time

No stopping
during times
shown on sign

Parking is limited to the
duration specified during
the days and times shown

Only loading may take
place at the times shown
for up to a maximum
duration of 20 mins

On the kerb or at the edge of the carriageway

Loading restrictions on roads other than Red Routes

Yellow marks on the kerb or at the edge of the carriageway indicate that loading or unloading is prohibited at the times shown on the nearby black and white plates. You may stop while passengers board or alight. If no days are indicated on the signs the restrictions are in force every day including Sundays and Bank Holidays.

ALWAYS CHECK THE TIMES SHOWN ON THE PLATES.

Lengths of road reserved for vehicles loading and unloading are indicated by a white 'bay' marking with the words 'Loading Only' and a sign with the white on blue 'trolley' symbol. This sign also shows whether loading and unloading is restricted to goods vehicles and the times at which the bay can be used. If no times or days are shown it may be used at any time. Vehicles may not park here if they are not loading or unloading.

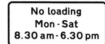

No loading or unloading
at any time

No loading or unloading
at the times shown

Loading bay

Other road markings

Keep entrance clear of stationary vehicles, even if picking up or setting down children

Warning of 'Give Way'
just ahead

Parking space reserved
for vehicles named

See Rule 243

See Rule 141

Box junction - See
Rule 174

Do not block that part of
the carriageway indicated

Indication of traffic lanes

Section Twelve

DOCUMENTS

The Essence:

1. The paperwork is important. If you don't get it right it will land you in trouble and it can cost you plenty.

2. The older the car and the younger the driver, the more the paperwork.

3. The most important aspect of this section relates to insurance. If your paperwork is not right you may be uninsured even if you have paid premiums to an insurance company. This is grossly irresponsible. What if you kill or injure someone, deprive their family of a livelihood or destroy their vehicle? Will you pay out of your own pocket? They might make you pay for the rest of your life. Insurance is to protect them and you from any stupidity on your part.

Insurance:
(1) All drivers, including newly qualified drivers, must have valid motor insurance.
(2) "Cover Note" is document confirming insurance has been agreed & is received before the Insurance Certificate.
(3) The legal minimum insurance = 3rd Party only = cover for injury to another person/ damage to someone's property/damage to other vehicles.
(4) Must show insurance certificate to police officer if asked for it.
(5) "£100 excess" = you must pay the first £100 of any claim.
(6) Max specified fine for driving without insurance = £5000.
(7) Before driving another's car, check the car is insured for your use.

MOT Certificate:
(1) Required for cars older than 3 years.
(2) Valid for 1 year after issue date.
(3) Drive without valid MOT = can invalidate insurance.
(4) Only time can drive car older than 3 years without MOT is when driving to appointment at MOT centre.
(5) Cannot renew road tax disc without valid MOT.

Police:
If police ask for docs but you not have them with you – may be asked to take to police station within 7 days.

Penalty Points:
6 penalty points within 2 years of passing practical test = re-apply for prov. licence + retake theory & practical test (i.e. go back to square 1)

Learners: -
(1) Must have signed valid provisional licence to drive on road.
(2) To supervise learner must be at least 21 years + hold full licence for at least 3 years.

DOCUMENTS

Vehicle Excise Duty (Road Tax):
(1) Must have valid insurance to renew.
(2) Must have MOT for vehicle older than 3 years.

Pass Plus Scheme:
(1) Created to improve basic driving skills & widen experience of newly qualified drivers.
(2) May reduce cost of insurance.

Statutory Off Road Notification (SORN):
A notification to DVLA that vehicle is not being used on the road. Lasts 12 months

Vehicle Registration Document:
Contains:
(1) Registered Keeper.
(2) Make of vehicle.
(3) Engine size.
Should update when move house & registered keeper is responsible for updating.

Licensing Authority: -
Must contact when:
(1) Change vehicle.
(2) Change name.
(3) Change permanent address.
(4) Health affects driving.
(5) Eyesight not meet set standard.

TEST TIPS:

1. This is boring stuff, but you have to know it. If you read through the previous page a few times you should remember enough to recognise the correct answers.

Section Thirteen

ACCIDENTS

The Essence:

1. This whole learner's licence/theory test/practical test process you are going through has one fundamental purpose – to reduce the risk of you having accidents.

2. It is impossible to overstate how dreadful the consequences of a motor accident can be. Lives are snuffed out, families are destroyed and individuals are crippled. At the very least, even the most minor "fender-bender" damages property.

3. If you are involved in a collision with anything or anyone as the driver of a moving vehicle the law requires you to stop. Common decency also requires this.

4. This section deals with how you handle the immediate consequences and aftermath of a collision. It covers safety and first aid matters in the first section and other more technical matters in the second section.

5. **Please pay attention to this – it could save someone's life.**

At the Scene:
(1) Do not put yourself at risk.
(2) First thing to do is warn other traffic e.g. by switching on hazard lights.
(3) Call emergency services promptly.
(4) Make sure engines are switched off.
(5) Get people who are not injured clear of the scene.
(6) Keep injured people warm & comfortable.
(7) Keep injured people calm by talking to them reassuringly.
(8) Make sure injured people are not left alone.
(9) Only move casualties if they are in continuing/further danger.
(10) If area is safe, should not move casualties – keep them in vehicle, particularly if back injuries suspected.

STOP!!!
If have collision while car is moving – you **must** stop at the scene.

Unconscious Casualty:
Checks:
(1) First priority is to check breathing and that airway is clear.
(2) Check breathing for at least 10 seconds.
(3) Stop any heavy bleeding.
(4) Check circulation i.e. heart beat.

Action if casualty has stopped breathing:
(1) Restore breathing by removing anything blocking mouth/ tilt head back to clear airway/pinch nostrils together/breathe into mouth (NB. small child - breathe gently into mouth).
(2) To maintain circulation, chest compressions should be given at the rate of 100 per minute to a depth of 4 to 5 cm.
(3) Always seek medical assistance when casualty is unconscious.

ACCIDENTS (1)

Shock:
(1) Warning signs = pale grey skin/ sweating.
(2) Reassure them constantly.
(3) Keep them warm.
(4) Avoid moving if possible.
(5) Avoid leaving them alone
(6) Do not offer cigarette/drink.

Bleeding:
(1) To stop – apply firm pressure to wound.
(2) Leg/arm wound – raise leg/arm to lessen bleeding.

Burns:
(1) Do not remove anything stuck to burn.
(2) Douse burn with clean, cool, non-toxic liquid.
(3) Cool burn for minimum of 10 minutes.

Motorcycle Crash:
Never remove motorcyclist's helmet unless it is essential – removal may result in more serious injury.

Breakdowns:

(1) Warning triangle - place 45 m from vehicle.

(2) Warning light on dash – check out problem quickly and safely.

(3) Level Crossing –
   a. Leave vehicle & get everyone clear;
   b. Telephone signal operator;
   c. Move vehicle if signal operator tells you to.

(4) Tyre Bursts –
   a. Pull up slowly/let vehicle roll to a stop at side of road
   b. Hold steering wheel firmly.

(5) Puncture on Motorway –
   a. Pull up on hard shoulder
   b. Use emergency phone to phone for assistance (when use phone will be asked for the number on the phone you are using/ details of yourself and your vehicle/whether you belong to motoring organisation.

Fire:

(1) Engine catch fire – phone fire brigade – do not try to deal with it yourself by lifting bonnet etc – dangerous!

(2) 2 safeguards against fire: carry fire extinguisher/ check out any strong smell of petrol.

(3) Catch fire in tunnel? – If car drivable - drive it out of tunnel if you can do so. If car not drivable – switch on hazard lights & try put fire out (if safe to do so)

Equipment for collisions:

(1) First aid kit.

(2) Fire extinguisher.

(3) Warning triangle.

ACCIDENTS (2)

Box/Luggage falls onto motorway:

Go to next emergency phone and inform police.

Do not try to deal with it yourself.

Information after Collision:-

(1) Other drivers name & address.

(2) Whether driver owns vehicle.

(3) Make & reg. no. of other vehicle.

(4) Details of other drivers insurance.

(5) If do not give name & address at time of collision – report to police ASAP or within 24 hrs.

Tunnels:

(1) Going through congested tunnel and you have to stop because of traffic in front – you keep a safe distance from the vehicle in front.

(2) Long tunnels may have Variable Message Signs to warn of incidents or congestion ahead.

(3) Remove sunglasses upon entering tunnels.

(4) Use dipped headlights.

(5) If break down/ have collision – switch on hazard lights, switch off engine & then go and call for help.

Documents:

After collision police may ask for production of:

(1) Driving licence.

(2) Insurance certificate.

(3) MOT Test certificate.

Section Fourteen

VEHICLE LOADING

The Essence:

1. Towing a trailer or carrying a heavy load on or in your vehicle creates stress for both the vehicle and the driver. Stability, steering, handling and stopping distances are all affected. It is more dangerous and caution is required.

2. Speed limits are reduced for towing and you are obliged by law to stay in the left hand lane.

3. Stabilisers, breakaway cables and other devices can be fitted to counteract the problems.

Trailers & Caravans:

(1) Do not exceed 60mph ever.

(2) Use only left & centre lanes on 3 lane motorway.

(3) "Snaking" from side to side? – slow down gradually by easing off the accelerator slowly.

(4) No passengers in trailer/caravan at any time.

(5) Fitting stabiliser to the tow bar helps vehicle handling, particularly in crosswind.

(6) Max nose weight of vehicle's tow ball? – look in vehicle handbook.

(7) A breakaway cable is an additional safety device.

VEHICLE LOADING

Tyres:

Inflate tyres to more than the recommended normal tyre pressure when:

(1) Driving fast for a long distance; and

(2) Carrying a heavy load.

Roof Racks:

(1) Loads must be securely fastened.

(2) Heavy load will reduce stability.

Overloading:

(1) Seriously affects both steering & handling.

(2) **Driver** is responsible for any overloading.

TEST TIPS:

1. A caravan is simply a large and cumbersome type of trailer. What applies to the one applies to the other.

2. Don't overlook this tiny section just because it is tacked on at the end. Every correct answer is worth the same to you in the test.

FACTS THAT DID NOT FIT

There are a few facts that you should know but which just didn't fit into any of the Study Patterns. Here they are:

1. A flashing amber light at a Pelican pedestrian crossing means you must give way to pedestrians already on the crossing.

2. A flashing blue beacon on a vehicle = emergency vehicle, i.e.:

   Ambulance
   Fire Engine
   Police patrol
   Bomb disposal
   Blood transfusion
   Mountain Rescue

   Pull over where safe to do so and give way.

3. A flashing green beacon on a vehicle = Doctor answering emergency call.

4. You may never park on a pedestrian crossing of any type.

5. The purpose of red routes is to ease traffic flow.

6. Signals on an ordinary car are given by the indicator lights and the break lights.

7. A "Help" pendant displayed on a vehicle = most likely a disabled person.